Plus

Physical Science

Light

by Abbie Dunne

CAPSTONE PRESS
a capstone imprint

Pebble Plus is published by Capstone Press,
1710 Roe Crest Drive, North Mankato, Minnesota 56003
www.mycapstone.com

Library of Congress Cataloging-in-Publication Data
Names: Dunne, Abbie, author.
Title: Light / by Abbie Dunne.
Description: North Mankato, Minnesota : Capstone Press, [2017] | Series:
   Pebble plus. Physical science | Audience: Ages 4-8. | Audience: K to
   grade 3. | Includes bibliographical references and index.
Identifiers: LCCN 2016005340 | ISBN 9781515709374 (library binding) | ISBN
   9781515709695 (pbk.) | ISBN 9781515711049 (ebook (pdf))
Subjects: LCSH: Light—Juvenile literature. | Color—Juvenile literature.
Classification: LCC QC360 .D86 2017 | DDC 535—dc23
LC record available at http://lccn.loc.gov/2016005340

Editorial Credits
Linda Staniford, editor; Veronica Scott, designer; Eric Gohl, media researcher;
Katy LaVigne, production specialist

Photo Credits
Shutterstock: cocoangel, 13, Gelpi JM, 5, iconizer, 20 (mug), J. Palys, 11, leolintang, 9, LiAndStudio, 19, Michael C. Gray, 15, Monticello, 20 (jar), Ron Dale, 20 (glass), Sabphoto, cover, S_E, 7, wizdata1, 17

Design Elements: Shutterstock

Note to Parents and Teachers
The Physical Science set supports national curriculum standards for science. This book introduces the concept of light. The images support early readers in understanding the text. The repetition of words and phrases helps early readers in understanding the text. This book also introduces early readers to subject-specific vocabulary words, which are defined in the Glossary section. Early readers may need assistance to read some words and to use the Table of Contents, Glossary, Read More, Internet Sites, Critical Thinking Using the Common Core, and Index sections of the book.

Printed and bound in China.
007701

Table of Contents

What is Light?

Light is energy that travels in a ray. Light bounces off things and goes into our eyes. This is how we see things.

Sources of Light

Light comes from many sources. The largest light source is the sun. The moon and stars make light too. So do lightbulbs, candles, and TVs.

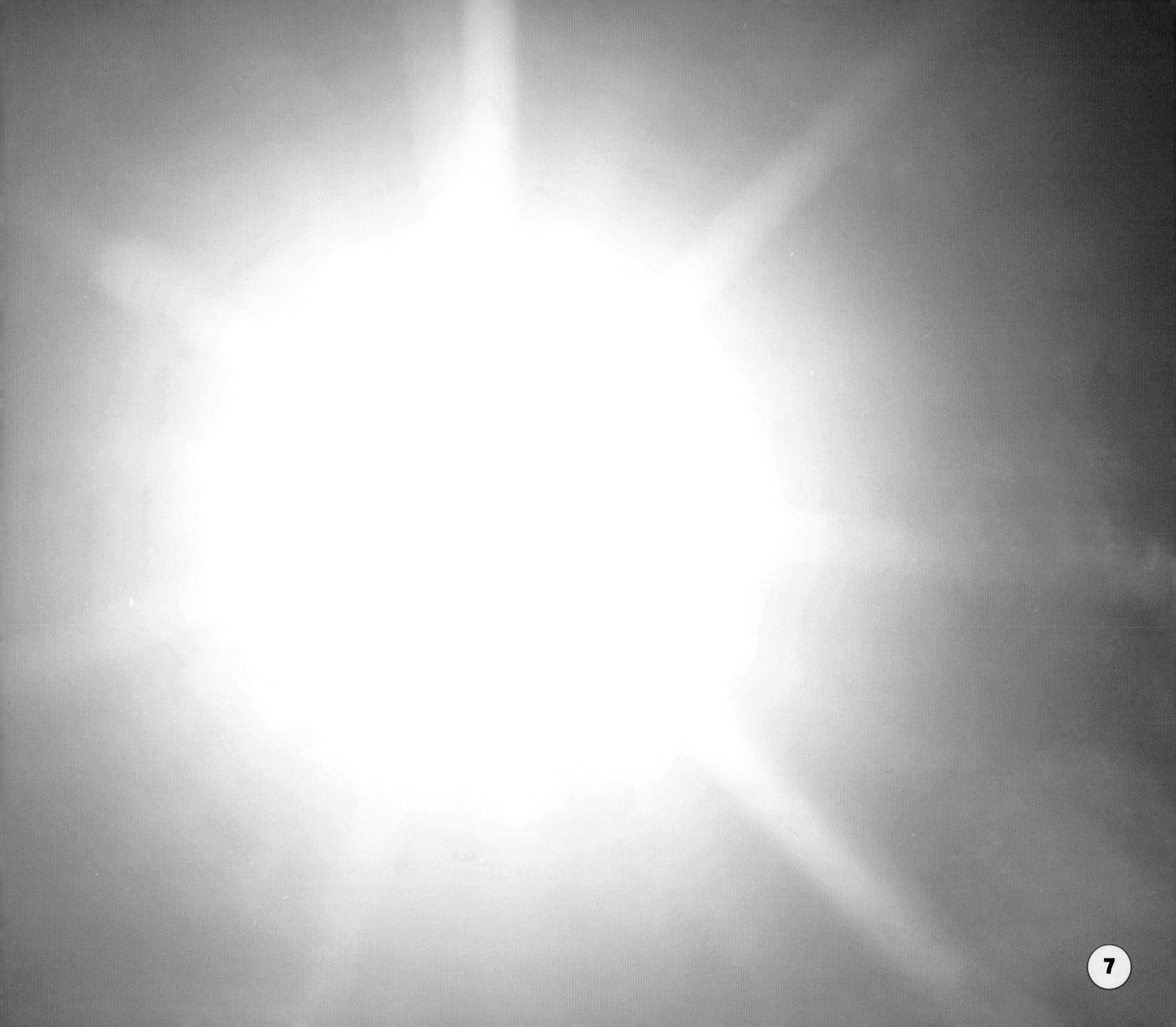

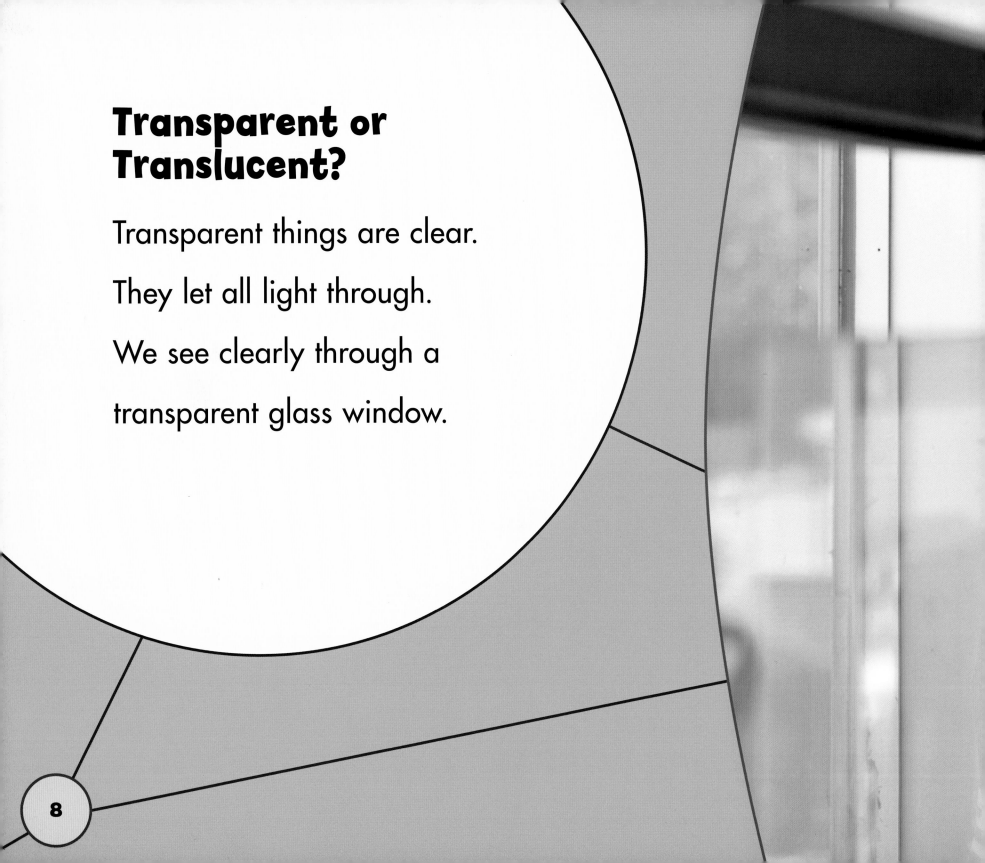

Transparent or Translucent?

Transparent things are clear.

They let all light through.

We see clearly through a transparent glass window.

Translucent things scatter some light. Things look blurry through colored glass because it is translucent.

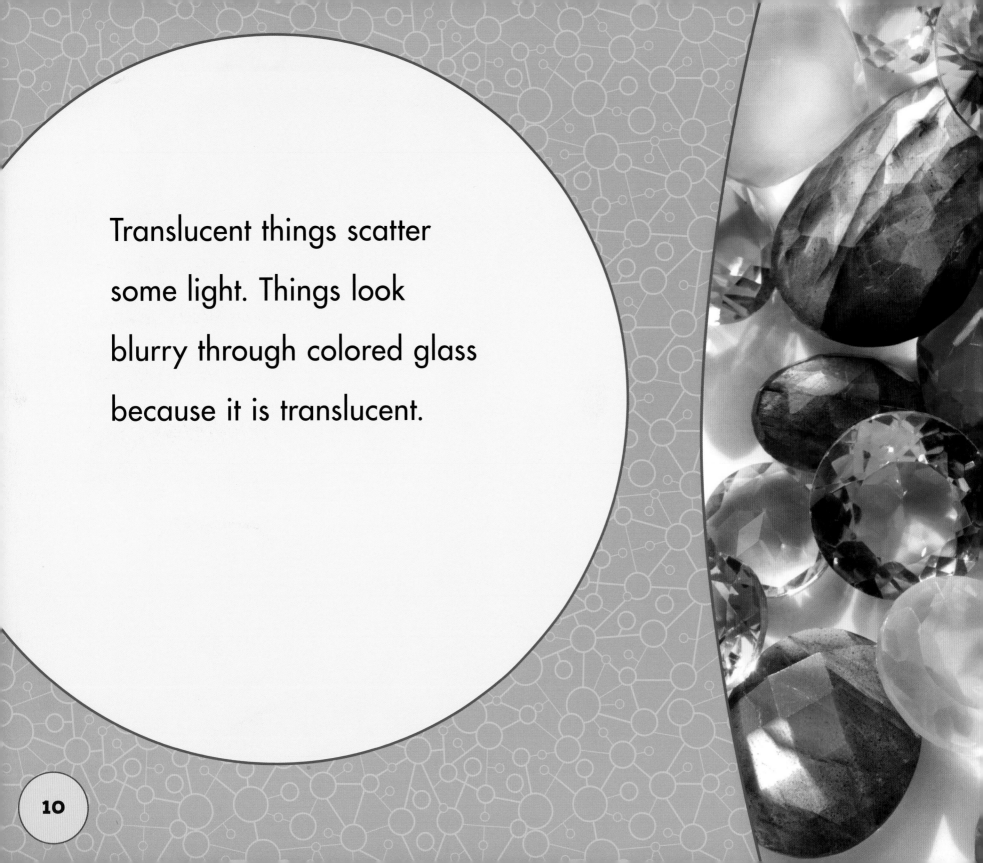

Blocking or Reflecting?

Some things, such as wood and rocks, don't let any light through. They are opaque. We can't see through these things.

Other things are shiny.
Light is bounced off of them,
or reflected. A mirror
reflects a lot of light.
You can see yourself in it.

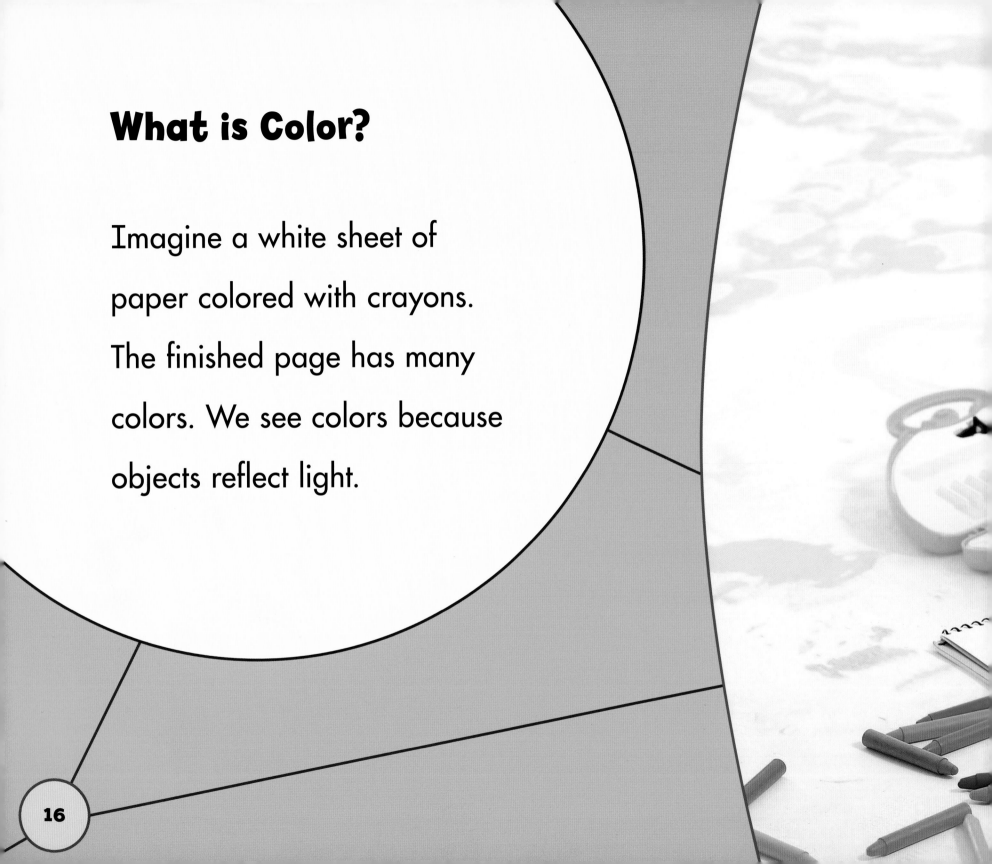

What is Color?

Imagine a white sheet of paper colored with crayons. The finished page has many colors. We see colors because objects reflect light.

Some light is reflected
off of an object. The color
light that reflects is the color
we see. Green light reflects off
of grass, so grass looks green.

Activity

Have you wondered what kinds of items make shadows?

Do this activity to find out which items make shadows and why.

What You Need

- 3 sheets of paper
- pencil
- book
- white index card
- objects that are transparent, translucent, and opaque
- flashlight
- pencil and paper for making notes
- digital camera or crayons and paper

translucent

transparent

opaque

What You Do

1. On one sheet of paper, write "transparent=light passes through."

2. Write "translucent=some light passes through" at the top of another sheet of paper.

3. Write "opaque=no light passes through" on the third sheet. Set aside.

4. Put the book on the table in front of you. Stand the index card against it.

5. Put the first object about an arm's length in front of the index card.

6. Turn on the flashlight. Shine the light on the front of the object.

7. See how much light shines through the object onto the card. Is there a shadow? Take notes.

8. Put the object on the piece of paper that describes it.

9. Repeat until all of your objects are sorted into the correct piles.

10. Draw a picture of the piles, or use a camera to take a picture of them.

What Do You Think?

Make a claim.

A claim is something you believe to be true.

What kinds of objects make shadows? Why? Use the results of the experiment to support your claim.

Glossary

opaque—letting no light pass through

ray—a line of light that beams out from something bright

reflect—to return light from an object

scatter—to separate something into smaller pieces and send it in many different directions

shadow—the dark shape made when something blocks light

source—the place where something begins

translucent—letting some light through

transparent—letting all light through

Read More

Boothroyd, Jennifer. *Light Makes Colors.* Light and Sound. Minneapolis, Minn.: Lerner Publications, 2015.

Lowery, Lawrence F. *Light and Color.* I Wonder Why. Arlington, Va.: National Science Teachers Association, 2014.

Pfeffer, Wendy. *Light is All Around Us.* Let's-Read-And-Find-Out-Science. New York: HarperCollins, 2014.

Internet Sites

FactHound offers a safe, fun way to find Internet sites related to this book. All of the sites on FactHound have been researched by our staff.

Here's all you do:

Visit www.facthound.com

Type in this code: 9781515709374

 Super-cool stuff!

Check out projects, games and lots more at
www.capstonekids.com

Critical Thinking Using the Common Core

1. Why can we see clearly through a transparent glass window?
   (Key Ideas and Details)

2. Wood and rocks are opaque. What does this mean?
   (Key Ideas and Details)

3. Grass looks green because green light reflects off of it.
   Why do you think a pumpkin looks orange?
   (Integration of Knowledge and Ideas)

Index